PRAYING THE ROSARY
WITH ST. JOHN PAUL II

PRAYING THE ROSARY
WITH ST. JOHN PAUL II

GRETCHEN R. CROWE

Our Sunday Visitor
Huntington, Indiana

Our Sunday Visitor Publishing Division
Our Sunday Visitor, Inc.
200 Noll Plaza
Huntington, IN 46750
1-800-348-2440

ISBN: 978-1-68192-305-5 (Inventory No. T1989)
eISBN: 978-1-68192-306-2
LCCN: 2019930318

Cover design: Tyler Ottinger
Cover art: Pope John Paul II, GRZEGORZ GALAZKA/BRIDGEMAN IMAGES and Madonna and Child Enthroned, FRA ANGELICO/ALAMY
Interior design: Amanda Falk
Interior art: Shutterstock, photos credited in caption section at end of book

PRINTED IN THE UNITED STATES OF AMERICA

For Joseph and Anne

CONTENTS

AUTHOR'S NOTE

"The Rosary is my favorite prayer. A marvelous prayer. Marvelous in its simplicity and its depth."

— Angelus, October 29, 1978

These were Pope St. John Paul II's first public words spoken as Holy Father on the prayer that would become a hallmark of his twenty-six-year papacy. His love for the Blessed Virgin Mary and for the Rosary would be responsible for inspiring generations of Catholics to a greater devotion to the Marian prayer. John Paul encouraged the faithful to recite a daily Rosary, and led by example through his own profound prayer life, reciting the full fifteen mysteries each day. His witness even had an impact on the future Pope Francis who, as Cardinal Jorge Mario Bergoglio of Buenos Aires, was so moved by John Paul's piety while reciting the Rosary that he, too, began to recite all of the mysteries of the Rosary daily — a practice that he continues.

Throughout his papacy, Pope John Paul II constantly reminded the faithful that it is through Mary and the Rosary that one is better able to know Jesus Christ. In that same first Angelus, he said, "Against the background of the words 'Ave Maria' there pass before the eyes of the soul the main episodes in the life of Jesus Christ. They are composed altogether of the joyful, sorrowful and glorious mysteries, and they put us in living communion with Jesus through — we could say — his Mother's heart."

John Paul II's devotion to the Rosary was so deep that he proclaimed a Year of the Rosary for the Church from October 2002 to October 2003. And he surprised the world yet more greatly when, at the same time, he offered for contemplation and consideration five additional Rosary mysteries: the Mysteries of Light, or Luminous Mysteries. In this change to what he called the "traditional pattern" of praying the Rosary, John Paul proposed including "the mysteries of Christ's public ministry between his Baptism and his Passion." He made this addition, he wrote, in order to "bring out fully the Christological depth of the Rosary" and to "contemplate important aspects of the person of Christ as the definitive revelation of God" (*Rosarium Virginis Mariae*, 19).

This little book is designed to help readers form a deeper relationship both with the Marian prayer and with the saint who loved it so much. Each mystery contains an excerpt from a talk or writing of John Paul II, as well as a short reflection on how the saint embodied the spiritual fruit that accompanies the mystery. The spiritual fruits are those provided by St. Louis de Montfort. Those accompanying each Luminous Mystery are my own creation, first published in my previous book, *Why the Rosary, Why Now?*

May our beloved Pope John Paul II lead you to a greater love of Jesus through his mother's heart.

Gretchen R. Crowe

FOREWORD

JOHN PAUL'S PRAYER
By Andreas Widmer

I'm often asked my key impression of Pope John Paul II, and I have always said without hesitation that of all his qualities, the most remarkable was his concentration during prayer.

It was one of the first things I noticed about him. Early in my tour of duty as a Swiss Guard, I was assigned to work an evening prayer service to be led by the pope. It was a relatively small gathering — perhaps just fifty or one hundred people. Enough for the crowd to make a strong recorded response to his lead, as the service was to be broadcast live on Vatican radio around the world.

From my vantage point, the Holy Father was in my direct line of vision as he knelt in front of the group of people that prayed with him. I had no appreciation for the specific prayer and had not prayed it since my First Communion: the Rosary. I observed him curiously. I could not help but notice how, as he prayed, he came to radiate peacefulness and a calm unlike what I had seen in anyone before. He became totally absorbed in his prayer — completely taken up.

I was perplexed. I sensed that he was not acting a part, though my mind kept going back to that possibility at first, so unlike anything I'd ever witnessed was his demeanor. At the same time, I was compelled to dismiss this thought, because his praying next to me was so affecting. I could *feel* his peace. He was present, yet I could tell that he was also in a spiritual place. I felt that the silence and the sounds took on an otherworldliness. How could that be mere performance on his part? He was not paying any attention to me or anyone in the crowd. He was just there, praying and being at peace. I remember clearly that in the end, all I knew was that whatever it was that he experienced — I wanted it!

I overheard him later say that prayer is a learned ability and that anyone can pray. Until that point I'd always viewed prayer as some sort of fantasy or fiction — purely imaginary. During that evening, John Paul II showed me this was not so. To him, prayer was an encounter with a real person, an exchange, listening, talking. It was emotional, gentle, loving, and consequential.

One day, the Holy Father gave me a Rosary. It was one of his famous rosaries with the Lello Scorzelli crucifix on it. He encouraged me: "Pray this prayer, it is my favorite prayer." A priest who worked in the Vatican noticed my curiosity and instructed me on how to pray the Rosary meditatively. It would take some time and practice to get the hang of it, but in my line of work, I had plenty of time for that, he said. So I began to pray, first once a day, then working my way up to a few times a day.

On one occasion I began to pray, and the words merged into a whole, the rhythm of the verses moving back and forth like the rhythmic waves of the ocean. As I went along with that rhythm, these waves swept over my head and engulfed me; it was as if I was under water, entering a complete, quiet, calm peace. I felt a presence I understood to be God. I was so shocked and afraid, my Rosary fell out of my hands and I quickly came out of my meditation. I couldn't believe it: God really existed! I had experienced him! There was no room for doubt any more. I was happy. Terrified, too, to be honest — but I was hooked. The draw of that incredible presence I experienced, and the intrigue of it, was greater than my fear. I wanted to spend more time in that place. I found I could not arrive at that place at will, but once in a while, with fidelity, it happened: The waves crashed over me, and I was submerged in quiet. I learned when this happened not to fear, but to stay longer, resting in the experience. It was wonderful, peaceful, and nourishing.

John Paul gave me the biggest treasure you can give to a person: prayer — an experience of God! He was a pope of prayer. Through this lovely volume on the Rosary, drawn from St. John Paul II's own meditations on the mysteries of the Rosary, Gretchen Crowe allows John Paul to offer you the same gift he once offered a green and skeptical young Swiss Guard. May it prove a blessing to all who use it.

Andreas E. Widmer is the director of the Art & Carlyse Ciocca Center for Principled Entrepreneurship at The Busch School of Business at Catholic University. He is also the author of The Pope & The CEO: Pope Saint John Paul II's Lessons to a Young Swiss Guard, *a book exploring leadership lessons that Widmer learned serving as a Swiss Guard protecting Pope John Paul II and refined during his career as a successful business executive.*

BIOGRAPHY

THE LIFE OF POPE ST. JOHN PAUL II
By Russell Shaw

Sometimes it seemed as if Pope St. John Paul II could do just about anything — do it well, in fact — if he simply set his mind to doing it. This impression of uncommon giftedness would by itself have been enough to give his pontificate its special aura.

You could sum him up something like this: charismatic contemplative, prophetic voice of orthodoxy, sophisticated intellectual with profound devotion to the Virgin Mary, poet and athlete, foe of communism and of Western "super development," philosopher and activist with an actor's flair. And finally, in those last, painful years of illness and decline, a figure in whom many saw a living icon of the suffering Christ.

Coming to the papacy after a long night of confusion and anxiety in the Church, Pope John Paul II set out to make things right. "Be not afraid," he reassured the crowd in St. Peter's Square right after his election. As vicar of Christ and servant of the servants of God, he took his own advice, pursuing policies reflecting uncommon faith and self-confidence for nearly twenty-seven years.

He had his critics. Some groused about his teaching on sexual morality, others about his insistence that the Church can't ordain women, or his continued requirement of celibacy for priests of the Western Church, or his centralized leadership. Sometimes he was blamed for intervening too much in local bishops' affairs; other times — as in the sexual abuse scandal — for not intervening enough.

In the end, though, the critics could take nothing away from either the remarkable force of his personality or his extraordinary achievements. Eamon Duffy calls his pontificate — third longest in history, exceeded only by Blessed Pius IX and, according to tradition, St. Peter — one of the "most momentous" ever for its impact on the Church and the world.

Karol Jozef Wojtyła was born in Wadowice, an industrial town near Krakow, on May 18, 1920, second son of Karol Wojytyla, a Polish army officer, and Emilia Kaczorowska Wojtyła. His mother died in 1929; his older brother, Edmund, a physician, in 1932; and his father in 1941.

Before World War II he studied philosophy at the Jagiellonian University. When the Nazi occupiers of Poland, seeking to stamp out Polish intellectual life, closed down the university, he worked in a quarry and a chemical plant while acting with an underground theater.

In October 1942, he enrolled in the clandestine seminary conducted by Cardinal Adam Sapieha of Krakow. Ordained November 1, 1946, he went to Rome to study at the Angelicum — the Dominicans' Pontifical Athenaeum of St. Thomas.

Returning to Krakow, he did pastoral work, served as a student chaplain, and continued his studies, receiving doctorates from the Jagiellonian in philosophy and theology. He then taught moral theology and ethics at the Catholic University of Lublin. He also carried on an active apostolate among young lay intellectuals and professionals. On July 4, 1958, during a kayaking trip with young friends, he got word that Pope Pius XII had named him auxiliary bishop of Krakow.

He attended all four sessions of the Second Vatican Council, speaking several times and helping write the council's Pastoral Constitution on the Church in the Modern World, Declaration on Religious Freedom, and Decree on the Means of Social Communication.

In 1960 he published *Love and Responsibility*, a book presenting Church teaching on sexuality and marriage that is said to have influenced Pope St. Paul VI's encyclical *Humanae Vitae*. (Human sexuality was a subject to which Wojtyła would return years later as pope in laying out a distinctive new "theology of the body" in a series of audience talks.)

On January 13, 1964, Paul VI appointed him archbishop of Krakow. In the years that followed, he took part regularly in assemblies of the Synod of Bishops, convened an archdiocesan synod in Krakow, traveled widely in Europe and North America, and even visited Australia, the Philippines, and New Guinea. Pope Paul named him a cardinal on June 26, 1967. His book *The Act-*

ing Person, a densely written philosophical study, was published in 1969. In Lent of 1976 he preached the annual retreat attended by Pope Paul and the Roman curia. The meditations were published in a book titled *A Sign of Contradiction*.

On October 16, 1978, at the conclave following the sudden death of Pope John Paul I, he was elected 263rd successor of St. Peter, making him the first non-Italian to hold the office since 1522, the first Pole ever, and the youngest pope since Pius IX. The long pontificate that followed had numerous highlights.

One of these was his role in the collapse of Soviet communism and the dissolution of the Soviet empire in Eastern Europe — events in which his name is often linked to the names of President Ronald Reagan and British Prime Minister Margaret Thatcher.

In June 1979, his first visit to Poland since his election sparked a huge upsurge of Polish patriotic and religious sentiment, with thirteen million people turning out to see him, hear him, and pray with him.

Years later he attributed the fall of Soviet communism largely to the reaction against "the spiritual void brought about by atheism." Perhaps he was recalling the day in 1979 when the congregation at a Mass he celebrated in Warsaw's Victory Square began shouting, "We want God." He also gave significant moral and material support to the Solidarity labor movement in its struggle with the Polish communist regime.

Poland was hardly the only place visited by this most-traveled of popes, who covered a million miles in 104 trips outside Italy in his personal program of global evangelization. Five times he came to the United States — twice to address the United Nations — and crisscrossing the nation.

John Paul was an ecumenical and interreligious innovator who, in Duffy's words, "did more than any single individual in the whole history of Christianity to reconcile Jews and Christians." Catholic-Orthodox reunion also was a special cause for him. His 1995 encyclical *Ut Unum Sint* took the unusual step of inviting other Christians' thinking on the role of the papacy.

His many writings as pope reflect his personalist philosophy and his roots in Vatican II. Along with important documents on the laity and the dignity of women, four of his encyclicals are considered particularly noteworthy: the social encyclical *Centesimus Annus* (1991), *Veritatis Splendor* (1993) on fundamental moral principles, *Evangelium Vitae* (1995) on life issues, and *Fides et Ratio* in 1998 on the link between philosophy and faith.

Insisting that both things — philosophy and faith — are needed as antidotes to contemporary postmodern relativism and skepticism, he wrote: "To believe it possible to know a universally valid truth is in no way to encourage intolerance; on the contrary, it is the essential condition for sincere and authentic dialogue between persons." Catholic author Robert Royal calls his message "vital for a world that has lost its faith in reason."

John Paul canonized 482 saints — more than all his predecessors combined — and beatified 1,338 others. The saints include Maximilian Kolbe, Edith Stein, Mary Faustina Kowalska, Katherine Drexel, Padre Pio of Pietrelcina, and Josemaría Escriva. John Paul also promulgated the revised Code of Canon Law, a project originating in the pontificate of John XXIII, and commissioned and approved the new *Catechism of the Catholic Church*, the Church's first general catechism in four hundred years.

On May 13, 1981, Pope John Paul was shot in St. Peter's Square by a Turkish gunman named Mehmet Ali Ağca, apparently acting on behalf of Bulgarian intelligence in a plot orchestrated by Soviet intelligence. After a long and difficult recovery, he resumed his strenuous schedule, but starting in the early 1990s, he suffered visibly from Parkinson's.

After his death on Saturday, April 2, 2005, the crowd in the square began shouting, "*Santo subito!*" — canonize him now. Nine years later, on April 27, 2014, Pope Francis formally declared him a saint.

This biography originally appeared in the OSV Newsweekly *on October 10, 2018, as "Pope St. John Paul II: Witness to the World."*

THE JOYFUL MYSTERIES

First Joyful Mystery

The Annunciation of the Lord

"Behold, I am the handmaid of the Lord.
May it be done to me according to your word."

— Luke 1:38

Spiritual Fruit: Humility

From the very beginning of his papacy, Pope St. John Paul II made a beautiful habit of kissing the ground upon arriving in every country to which he traveled. It was a gesture learned from one of his spiritual heroes, St. John Vianney. Kissing the ground was a sign of great humility, an action that conveyed respect and affection, and which showed him to be at the faithful service of the people he had come to visit.

READ: LUKE 1:26–38
REFLECT WITH ST. JOHN PAUL II

The divine messenger says to (Mary): "Do not be afraid, Mary, for you have found favor with God. And behold, you will conceive in your womb and bear a son, and you shall call his name Jesus. He will be great, and will be called the Son of the Most High" (Lk 1:30–32). And when the Virgin, disturbed by that extraordinary greeting, asks: "How shall this be, since I have no husband?" she receives from the angel the confirmation and explanation of the preceding words. Gabriel says to her: "The Holy Spirit will come upon you, and the power of the Most High will overshadow you; therefore the child to be born will be called holy, the Son of God" (Lk 1:35).

The Annunciation, therefore, is the revelation of the mystery of the Incarnation at the very beginning of its fulfillment on earth. God's salvific giving of himself and his life, in some way to all creation but directly to man, reaches one of its high points in the mystery of the Incarnation. This is indeed a high point among all the gifts of grace conferred in the history of man and of the universe: Mary is "full of grace," because it is precisely in her that the Incarnation of the Word, the hypostatic union of the Son of God with human nature, is accomplished and fulfilled. As the Council says, Mary is "the Mother of the Son of God. As a result she is also the favorite daughter of the Father and the temple of the Holy Spirit. Because of this gift of sublime grace, she far surpasses all other creatures, both in heaven and on earth."

— *Redemptoris Mater*, No. 9, Encyclical, March 25, 1987

SECOND JOYFUL MYSTERY

The Visitation

"When Elizabeth heard Mary's greeting, the infant leaped in her womb, and Elizabeth, filled with the holy Spirit, cried out in a loud voice and said, 'Most blessed are you among women, and blessed is the fruit of your womb.'"

— Luke 1:41–42

Spiritual Fruit: Love of neighbor

St. John Paul II had a deep, lasting love of neighbor, and this virtue was exemplified on the worldwide stage when he chose not only to forgive the gunman who gravely wounded him in 1981, but to visit and speak with him in person as "a brother whom I have forgiven and who enjoys my confidence."

READ: LUKE 1:39–56
REFLECT WITH ST. JOHN PAUL II

With this greeting, the elderly Elizabeth exalts her young kinswoman Mary, who has come, humble and modest, to help her. Under the impulse of the Holy Spirit, the mother of the Baptist is the first in the history of the Church to begin to proclaim the marvels that God has brought about in the girl from Nazareth, and sees fully realized in Mary *the bliss of faith*, because she has believed there would be a fulfillment of what was spoken to her from the Lord. … (The) feast of the Visitation presents to us another aspect of Mary's inner life: her attitude of *humble service* and *disinterested love* for those in need. She has just heard from the Angel

Gabriel of the state of her kinswoman Elizabeth, and at once she sets out for the hills "in haste" to reach a city of Judah, the present-day "Ain Karem." The meeting of the two Mothers is also the meeting between the Forerunner and the Messiah, who, through his Mother, begins to operate salvation by making John the Baptist leap with joy when still in his mother's womb. ... "Joyful in hope": the atmosphere that pervades the evangelical episode of the Visitation is *joy*: the mystery of the Visitation is a *mystery of joy*. John the Baptist exults with joy in the womb of St. Elizabeth; the latter, rejoicing in the gift of motherhood, bursts out into blessings of the Lord; Mary pours forth the "Magnificat," a hymn overflowing with Messianic joy.

But what is the mysterious, hidden source of this joy? It is Jesus, whom Mary has already conceived thanks to the Holy Spirit, and who is already beginning to defeat what is the root of fear, anguish and sadness: sin, the most humiliating slavery for man.

— Homily, May 31, 1979

THIRD JOYFUL MYSTERY

The Nativity of the Lord

"For today in the city of David a savior has been born for you who is Messiah and Lord."

— Luke 2:11

Spiritual Fruit: Love of poverty and of the poor

St. John Paul II had a great detachment from the things of this world, which allowed him to stay close to Christ. And he possessed a deep awareness of the plight of the poor, writing, "Love for others, and in the first place love for the poor, in whom the Church sees Christ himself, is made concrete in the promotion of justice. Justice will never be fully attained unless people see in the poor person, who is asking for help in order to survive, not an annoyance or a burden, but an opportunity for showing kindness and a chance for greater enrichment."

READ: LUKE 2:1–20
REFLECT WITH ST. JOHN PAUL II

"You will find a babe wrapped in swaddling cloths and lying in a manger" (Lk 2:12). The Child laid in a lowly manger: this is God's sign. The centuries and the millennia pass, but the sign remains, and it remains valid for us too — the men and women of the third millennium. It is a sign of hope for the whole human family; a sign of peace for those suffering from conflicts of every kind; a sign of freedom for the poor and oppressed; a sign of mercy for those caught up in the vicious circle of sin; a sign of love and consolation for those who feel lonely and abandoned. A small and fragile sign, a humble and quiet sign, but one filled with the power of God who out of love became man.

Lord Jesus, together with the shepherds we draw near to your Crib. We contemplate you, wrapped in swaddling cloths and lying in the manger. O Babe of Bethlehem, we adore you in silence with Mary, your ever-Virgin Mother. To you be glory and praise for ever, Divine Savior of the World! Amen.

— Homily for Christmas Midnight Mass, December 24, 2002

FOURTH JOYFUL MYSTERY

The Presentation of the Lord

"Behold, this child is destined for the fall and rise of many in Israel, and to be a sign that will be contradicted (and you yourself a sword will pierce) so that the thoughts of many hearts may be revealed."

— Luke 2:34–35

Spiritual Fruit: Wisdom and purity of heart and body

During the Sermon on the Mount, Jesus instructs the apostles on eight Beatitudes, including, "Blessed are the clean of heart, for they will see God" (Mt 5:8). Throughout his life, St. John Paul II strove for purity of heart and body — wholeheartedly desiring to follow Christ and to do his will. Striving for total union with the Lord defined his life, resulting in the holiness that culminated in his canonization.

READ: LUKE 2:22–38
REFLECT WITH ST. JOHN PAUL II

Even if no one was waiting for Joseph and Mary when they arrived hidden among the people at the temple in Jerusalem with the baby Jesus, something most unusual occurs. Here they meet persons guided by the Holy Spirit … Simeon and Anna: a man and a woman, representatives of the Old Covenant, who, in a certain sense, had lived their whole lives for the moment when the temple of Jerusalem would be visited by the expected Messiah. Simeon and Anna understand that the moment has come at last, and reassured by the meeting, they can face the last phase of their life with peaceful hearts: "Lord, now let your servant depart in peace, according to your word; for my eyes have seen your salvation" (Lk 2:29–30). At this discreet encounter, the words and actions effectively express the reality of the event taking place. The coming of the Messiah has not passed unobserved. It was recognized through the penetrating gaze of faith, which the elderly Simeon expresses in his moving words.

— Homily, Feast of the Presentation, February 2, 1997

FIFTH JOYFUL MYSTERY

The Finding of the Child Jesus in the Temple

*"Why were you looking for me? Did you not know
that I must be in my Father's house?"*

— Luke 2:49

Spiritual Fruit: Conversion of sinners, piety

Pope John Paul II had a heart that yearned for God, evident through his frequent prayer. Every day, he faithfully prayed the Liturgy of the Hours, celebrated Mass, spent time in Eucharistic Adoration, and prayed Rosaries. He also did much of his writing while in the presence of the Blessed Sacrament. As a close adviser once said: "He was a man in continuous dialogue with Our Lord, with the Mother of God."

READ: LUKE 2:41–52
REFLECT WITH ST. JOHN PAUL II

This passage seems to contrast with Luke's note that Jesus was obedient to Joseph and Mary (cf. 2:51). But, if one looks closely, here he seems to put himself in a conscious and almost deliberate antithesis to his normal state as son, unexpectedly causing a definite separation from Mary and Joseph. As his rule of conduct, Jesus states that he belongs only to the Father and does not mention the ties to his earthly family. Jesus' behavior seemed very unusual. Through this episode, Jesus prepares his Mother for the mystery of the Redemption. During those three dramatic days when the Son withdraws from them to stay in the temple, Mary and Joseph experience an anticipation of the triduum of his Passion, Death and Resurrection. Letting his Mother and Joseph depart for Galilee without telling them of his intention to stay behind in Jerusalem, Jesus brings them into the mystery of that suffering which leads to joy, anticipating what he would later accomplish with his disciples through the announcement of his Passover. … He takes the role of teacher, as he will later do in his public life, speaking words that arouse admiration: "And all who heard him were astounded at his understanding and his answers" (2:47). Revealing a wisdom that amazes his listeners, he begins to practice the art of dialogue that will be a characteristic of his saving mission.

— General Audience, January 15, 1997

THE LUMINOUS
MYSTERIES

FIRST LUMINOUS MYSTERY

The Baptism in the Jordan

"And a voice came from the heavens, saying, 'This is my beloved Son, with whom I am well pleased.'"

— Matthew 3:17

Spiritual Fruit: For obedience and vocation

When Father Karol Wojtyla was first named auxiliary bishop of Krakow, he was on a kayaking trip with his friends. He was summoned to Warsaw with no explanation. He set off immediately, having to flag down a milk truck on the way and ride amid the containers. After meeting with the cardinal there, he spent the next several hours prostrate in front of the Blessed Sacrament, saying he had "a lot to talk about with the Lord." Two and a half months later, he was ordained a bishop.

READ: MATTHEW 3:13–17
REFLECT WITH ST. JOHN PAUL II

"Seek the Lord while he may be found, call upon him while he is near" (Is 55:6). These words from the second part of the Book of Isaiah ring out on this Sunday that ends the Christmas season. They are an invitation to go more deeply into the meaning for us of today's Feast, the Baptism of the Lord. In spirit let us return to the banks of the Jordan where John the Baptist administered a Baptism of repentance, exhorting to conversion. Coming up to the Precursor is Jesus, and with his presence he transformed that gesture of repentance into a solemn manifestation of his divinity. A voice suddenly comes from heaven: *"You are my beloved Son; in you I am well pleased"* (Mk 1:11) and, in the form of a dove, the Spirit descends upon Jesus. In that extraordinary event, John saw realized (*sic*) what had been said about the Messiah born in Bethlehem, adored by the shepherds and the Magi. He was the very One foretold by the prophets, the beloved Son of the Father; we must seek him while he can be found and call upon him while he is at hand. In Baptism every Christian personally meets him; he is inserted into the mystery of Christ's death and resurrection and receives a new life, which is the life of God. What a great gift and what a great responsibility! The liturgy today invites us to draw water *"with joy at the fountain of salvation"* (Is 12:3); it exhorts us to relive our Baptism, giving thanks for the great gifts received.

— Homily, Feast of the Baptism of the Lord, January 12, 2003

Second Luminous Mystery

The Wedding at Cana

"His mother said to the servers, 'Do whatever he tells you.'"

—John 2:5

Spiritual Fruit: For a manifestation of God in the world through our actions, particularly in marriage and family life

As a young priest in Communist Poland, Father Karol Wojtyla, the future Pope John Paul II, had a group of close friends for whom he served as mentor, counselor, and confidant. He counseled them frequently on many subjects, including marital chastity and sexual love, bringing them to a deeper understanding of the Church's faith concerning responsible love, a topic on which he would preach and teach so eloquently and memorably throughout his pontificate, particularly through his theology of the body.

READ: JOHN 2:1–12
REFLECT WITH ST. JOHN PAUL II

At Cana in Galilee there is shown only one concrete aspect of human need, apparently a small one of little importance ("They have no wine"). But it has a symbolic value: this coming to the aid of human needs means, at the same time, bringing those needs within the radius of Christ's messianic mission and salvific power. Thus there is a mediation: Mary places herself between her Son and mankind in the reality of their wants, needs and sufferings. She puts herself "in the middle," that is to say she acts as a mediatrix not as an outsider, but in her position as mother. She knows that as such she can point out to her Son the needs of mankind, and in fact, she "has the right" to do so. Her mediation is thus in the nature of intercession: Mary "intercedes" for mankind. And that is not all. As a mother she also wishes the messianic power of her Son to be manifested, that salvific power of his which is meant to help man in his misfortunes, to free him from the evil which in various forms and degrees weighs heavily upon his life. Precisely as the Prophet Isaiah had foretold about the Messiah in the famous passage which Jesus quoted before his fellow townsfolk in Nazareth: "To preach good news to the poor … to proclaim release to the captives and recovering of sight to the blind … " (cf. Lk 4:18). Another essential element of Mary's maternal task is found in her words to the servants: "Do whatever he tells you." The Mother of Christ presents herself as the spokeswoman of her Son's will, pointing out those things which must be done so that the salvific power of the Messiah may be manifested. At Cana, thanks to the intercession of Mary and the obedience of the servants, Jesus begins "his hour." At Cana Mary appears as believing in Jesus. Her faith evokes his first "sign" and helps to kindle the faith of the disciples.

— *Redemptoris Mater*, No. 21, Encyclical, March 25, 1987

THIRD LUMINOUS MYSTERY

The Proclamation of the Kingdom

"This is the time of fulfillment. The kingdom of God is at hand. Repent, and believe in the gospel."

— Mark 1:15

Spiritual Fruit: For an evangelistic spirit

During his time as pope, John Paul II embarked on more trips than all of his predecessors put together — a remarkable 104 visits to 129 countries. His travels allowed him to bring the Gospel to the world, connecting with those he met in a personal and engaging manner. He desired to inspire others to "be not afraid" of proclaiming Christ.

READ: MATTHEW 4:23–25
REFLECT WITH ST. JOHN PAUL II

"Jesus came into Galilee, preaching the gospel of God and saying, 'The time is fulfilled, and the kingdom of God is at hand; repent and believe in the gospel'" (Mk 1:15). These are the first words Jesus spoke to the crowd: they contain the heart of his Gospel of hope and salvation, the proclamation of God's kingdom. From that moment on, as the Evangelists note, Jesus "went about all Galilee, teaching in their synagogues and preaching the gospel of the kingdom and healing every disease and every infirmity among the people" (Mt 4:23; cf. Lk 8:1). The Apostles followed in his footsteps and with them Paul, the Apostle to the Gentiles, called to "preach the kingdom of God" among the nations even to the capital of the Roman Empire (cf. Acts 20:25; 28:23, 31). … Jesus asks us "to seek" actively "the kingdom of God and his righteousness" and to make this search our primary concern (Mt 6: 33). To those who "supposed that the kingdom of God was to appear immediately" (Lk 19:11), he prescribed an active attitude instead of passive waiting, telling them the parable of the ten pounds to be used productively (cf. Lk 19:12–27). For his part, the Apostle Paul states that "the kingdom of God does not mean food and drink but righteousness" (Rom 14:17) above all, and urges the faithful to put their members at the service of righteousness for sanctification (cf. Rom 6:13, 19).

The human person is thus called to work with his hands, mind and heart for the coming of God's kingdom into the world. This is especially true of those who are called to the apostolate and are, as St. Paul says, "fellow workers for the kingdom of God" (Col 4:11), but it is also true of every human person.

— General Audience, December 6, 2000

FOURTH LUMINOUS MYSTERY

The Transfiguration

*"And he was transfigured before them; his face shone
like the sun and his clothes became white as light."*

— Matthew 17:2

Spiritual Fruit: For ongoing conversion to Christ

In all that he did, St. John Paul II followed Jesus Christ, and his great witness and love inspired others to do the same. His example of charity, humility, love of neighbor, and love of God has inspired countless individuals — especially young people — to ongoing conversion to Jesus Christ, and his impact continues today.

READ: MATTHEW 17:1–8
REFLECT WITH ST. JOHN PAUL II

The event of the Transfiguration marks a decisive moment in the ministry of Jesus. It is a revelatory event which strengthens the faith in the disciples' hearts, prepares them for the tragedy of the Cross and prefigures the glory of the Resurrection. This mystery is constantly relived by the Church, the people on its way to the eschatological encounter with its Lord. Like the three chosen disciples, the Church contemplates the transfigured face of Christ in order to be confirmed in faith and to avoid being dismayed at his disfigured face on the Cross. In both cases, she is the Bride before her Spouse, sharing in his mystery and surrounded by his light. This light shines on all the Church's children. *All are equally called to follow Christ*, to discover in him the ultimate meaning of their lives, until they are able to say with the Apostle: "For to me to live is Christ" (Phil 1:21). ... The three disciples caught up in ecstasy hear the Father's call to listen to Christ, to place all their trust in him, to make him the center of their lives. The words from on high give new depth to the invitation by which Jesus himself, at the beginning of his public life, called them to follow him, to leave their ordinary lives behind and to enter into a close relationship to him.

— *Vita Consecrata*, Apostolic Exhortation, March 25, 1996

Fifth Luminous Mystery

The Institution of the Eucharist

"While they were eating, Jesus took bread, said the blessing, broke it, and giving it to his disciples said, 'Take and eat; this is my body.' Then he took a cup, gave thanks, and gave it to them, saying, 'Drink from it, all of you, for this is my blood of the covenant, which will be shed on behalf of many for the forgiveness of sins.'"

— Matthew 26:26–28

Spiritual Fruit: For a deeper love of and reverence
for the Blessed Sacrament

St. John Paul II had a great, lifelong love of the Eucharist, and one of his final acts was meant to rekindle love for the Blessed Sacrament in the hearts of the faithful. John Paul directed the Church to dedicate an entire year — October 2004 to October 2005 — to deeper reflection on, and growth in, love of the Eucharist.

READ: MATTHEW 26:26–30
REFLECT WITH ST. JOHN PAUL II

The Church was born of the paschal mystery. For this very reason the Eucharist, which is in an outstanding way the sacrament of the paschal mystery, *stands at the center of the Church's life*. This is already clear from the earliest images of the Church found in the Acts of the Apostles: "They devoted themselves to the Apostles' teaching and fellowship, to the breaking of bread and the prayers" (2:42). The "breaking of the bread" refers to the Eucharist. Two thousand years later, we continue to relive that primordial image of the Church. At every celebration of the Eucharist, we are spiritually brought back to the paschal Triduum: to the events of the evening of Holy Thursday, to the Last Supper and to what followed it. The institution of the Eucharist sacramentally anticipated the events which were about to take place, beginning with the agony in Gethsemane. Once again we see Jesus as he leaves the Upper Room, descends with his disciples to the Kidron valley and goes to the Garden of Olives. Even today that Garden shelters some very ancient olive trees. Perhaps they witnessed what happened beneath their shade that evening, when Christ in prayer was filled with anguish "and his sweat became like drops of blood falling down upon the ground" (cf. Lk 22:44). The blood which shortly before he had given to the Church as the drink of salvation in the sacrament of the Eucharist, *began to be shed*; its outpouring would then be completed on Golgotha to become the means of our redemption: "Christ … as high priest of the good things to come … entered once for all into the Holy Place, taking not the blood of goats and calves but his own blood, thus securing an eternal redemption" (Heb 9:11–12).

— *Ecclesia de Eucharistia*, Encyclical, April 13, 2003

THE SORROWFUL MYSTERIES

FIRST SORROWFUL MYSTERY

The Agony in the Garden

"He advanced a little and fell prostrate in prayer,
saying, 'My Father, if it is possible, let this cup pass
from me; yet, not as I will, but as you will.'"

— Matthew 26:39

Spiritual Fruit: Conformity to God's will

When St. John Paul II was elected pope on October 16, 1978, he responded with the greatest obedience, wholeheartedly accepting God's will for his life. Here are the very words he spoke upon accepting the papal responsibility, which reflect his incredible surrender to God's will: "In the obedience of faith before Christ my Lord, abandoning myself to the Mother of Christ and the Church, and conscious of the great difficulties, *accepto*."

READ: MATTHEW 26:36–46
REFLECT WITH ST. JOHN PAUL II

We read in the Letter to the Hebrews: "In the days when he was in the flesh, (Christ) offered prayers and supplications with loud cries and tears to God, who was able to save him from death" (Heb 5:7). These words have special application to the agony in the Garden of Gethsemane when he prayed: "My Father, if it is possible, let this cup pass me by" (Mt 26:39–42). The author of the Letter to the Hebrews immediately adds that Christ "was heard because of his reverence" (Heb 5:7). Yes he was heard. He had said, "not as I will, but as you will" (Mt 26:39). And so it came to pass. The agony of Christ was, and still is, the mystery of his obedience to the Father. *At Gethsemane. On Calvary.* "Son though he was," the text continues, "he learned obedience from what he suffered" (Heb 5:8). This includes Christ's obedience even unto death — the perfect sacrifice of Redemption. "And when perfected, he became the source of eternal salvation for all who obey him" (Ibid. 5:9).

— Homily at the Los Angeles Coliseum during apostolic journey to the United States and Canada, September 15, 1987

SECOND SORROWFUL MYSTERY

The Scourging at the Pillar

"Then Pilate took Jesus and had him scourged."

— John 19:1

Spiritual Fruit: Grace to mortify our senses (purity)

It was reported widely after Pope John Paul II's death that the saint had practiced strict acts of penance, including fasting and self-mortification. The postulator of his cause for canonization reported that the pope had used self-mortification "both to affirm the primacy of God and as an instrument for perfecting himself."

READ: JOHN 18:28–19:1
REFLECT WITH ST. JOHN PAUL II

For many people the scourging of the Lord became the decisive reason for their determination to break the bonds of sin, the reason for mortifying the concupiscence of the flesh, for turning their desires towards the noble and the holy. "I treat my body sternly and keep it under control" (1 Cor 9:27) wrote St. Paul, and many others have said the same thing and stressed it by their behavior. "The flesh has desires that run counter to those of the spirit" (Gal 5:17). "If you live according to the flesh you will die; but if through the spirit you put to death the impulses of the body you will live" (Rom 8:13).

— *Sign of Contradiction*, Meditation on the Sorrowful Mysteries

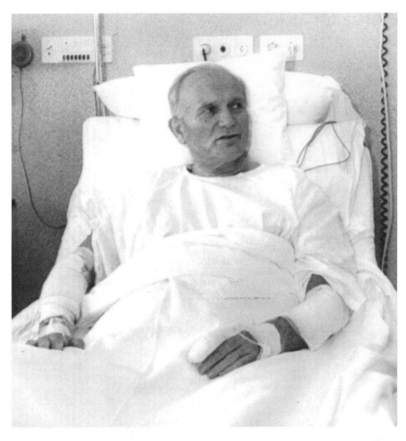

THIRD SORROWFUL MYSTERY

The Crowning with Thorns

*"Weaving a crown out of thorns, they placed it on his head,
and a reed in his right hand. And kneeling before him,
they mocked him, saying, 'Hail, King of the Jews!'"*

— Matthew 27:29

Spiritual Fruit: Deep contempt of the world

In many ways, St. John Paul II was countercultural because he viewed issues and events through the lens of faith and not the ways of the world. And he encouraged all who followed Christ to view the world similarly. Perhaps this was never more evident than in his consistent and frequent advocacy of the dignity of the human person, from conception to natural death. John Paul called the world to a different way of thinking — a way that prioritized the most vulnerable over the powerful and the weak over the strong.

READ: MATTHEW 27:27–31
REFLECT WITH ST. JOHN PAUL II

The torture inflicted on the Savior's head was a terrible one. It is an unforgettable torture, this one chosen by the soldiers for their mockery of the king of the Jews. The crown of thorns on the head of the condemned man whom Pilate had been unable to save from the crowd (cf. Mt 27:11–26) was particularly significant. Pilate had him brought out for the crowd to see in just that condition, crowned with thorns; he showed them all his humiliation and said: "Here is the man" (Jn 19:5). ... Precisely. All the kingliness of man, all man's dignity — which Jesus came to express and renew — are here summed up in him. Now it is well known that this is a kingliness that is frequently overpowered, hurled to the ground and thrust deep into the mud. It is also well-known that this is a dignity that is subjected to many kinds of humiliation. We are reminded by the second Vatican Council ... that Jesus came in order to reveal the kingliness of man. And here, visible to the whole of humanity, stands Jesus crowned with thorns! The price paid for dignity is the blood of the Son of God!

— *Sign of Contradiction*, Meditation on the Sorrowful Mysteries

FOURTH SORROWFUL MYSTERY

Jesus Carries His Cross

"A large crowd of people followed Jesus, including many women who mourned and lamented him."

— Luke 23:27

Spiritual Fruit: Patience in carrying our cross

Suffering was a significant part of Pope St. John Paul II's life, particularly in his final years as he battled Parkinson's disease. This disease must have been a particular trial for the former athlete who had once been full of vigor. But through infirmity and illness, John Paul displayed a perseverance and humility that was nothing short of beautiful. He offered a true witness to bearing one's cross with patience and purpose.

READ: LUKE 23:26–32
REFLECT WITH ST. JOHN PAUL II

The cross. The instrument of a shameful death. It was not lawful to condemn a Roman citizen to death by crucifixion: it was too humiliating. The moment that Jesus of Nazareth took up the Cross in order to carry it to Calvary marked a turning-point in the history of the cross. The symbol of a shameful death, reserved for the lowest classes, the cross *becomes a key*. From now on, with the help of this key, man will open the door of the deepest mystery of God.

Through Christ's acceptance of the Cross, the instrument of his own self-emptying, men will come to know that *God is love*. Love without limits: "God so loved the world that he gave his only Son, that whoever believes in him should not perish but have eternal life" (Jn 3:16). This truth about God was revealed in the Cross. Could it not have been revealed in some other way? Perhaps. But God chose the Cross. The Father chose the Cross for his Son, and his Son shouldered it, carried it to Mount Calvary and on it offered his life. "In the Cross there is suffering, in the Cross there is salvation, in the Cross there is a lesson of love. O God, he who once has understood you, desires nothing else, seeks nothing else" (Polish Lenten hymn). The Cross is the sign of a love without limits!

— Stations of the Cross at the Colosseum, Good Friday, 2000

FIFTH SORROWFUL MYSTERY

The Crucifixion

"Jesus cried out in a loud voice, 'Father, into your hands I commend my spirit'; and when he had said this he breathed his last."

— Luke 23:46

Spiritual Fruit: Great horror of sin, love
of the cross, grace for a holy death

The final words of St. John Paul II were spoken on his death-bed, hours before he passed away. They were uttered in his native Polish: "Allow me to depart to the house of the Father." After years of faithfully carrying out his ministry as successor of Peter amid great suffering, he humbly handed over his spirit to the Lord, seeking him anew at the end of life as he had done each and every day.

READ: LUKE 23:33–49
REFLECT WITH ST. JOHN PAUL II

Why are the Cross and the Crucified One the doorway to eternal life? Because in him — Christ crucified — is manifested to the full the love of God for the world, for man. In … conversation with Nicodemus, Christ says: "God loved the world so much that he gave his only Son, so that everyone who believes in him may not be lost but may have eternal life. For God sent his Son into the world, not to condemn the world, but so that through him the world might be saved" (Jn 3:16–17). The salvific lifting up of the Son of God on the Cross has its eternal source in love. This is the love of the Father that sends the Son; he gives his Son for the salvation of the world. And at the same time it is the love of the Son who does not "judge" the world, but gives himself for the love of the Father and for the salvation of the world. Giving himself to the Father through the Sacrifice of the Cross, he gives himself at the same time to the world: to each person and to the whole of humanity. The Cross contains in itself the mystery of salvation, because, in the Cross, Love is lifted up. This is the lifting up of Love to the supreme point in the history of the world: in the Cross Love is lifted up and the Cross is at the same time lifted up through Love. And from the height of the Cross, love comes down to us. Yes: "The Cross is the most profound condescension of God to man. … The Cross is like a touch of eternal love upon the most painful wounds of man's existence" (*Dives in Misericordia*, 8).

— Homily, Feast of the Triumph of the Cross, Halifax, apostolic journey to Canada, September 14, 1984

THE GLORIOUS MYSTERIES

FIRST GLORIOUS MYSTERY

The Resurrection of the Lord

"He is not here, but he has been raised."
— Luke 24:6

Spiritual Fruit: For a lively faith

Pope St. John Paul II was a gifted teacher, and he was especially gifted when it came to teaching on matters of doctrine. His arguments were clear and compelling, and always rooted in Scripture and Tradition. Through his clarity and consistency, despite facing much resistance at times, he helped all who encountered him better know and understand the teachings of Christ and his Church.

READ: LUKE 24:1–12
REFLECT WITH ST. JOHN PAUL II

The Resurrection of Jesus is the fundamental event upon which Christian faith rests (cf. 1 Cor 15:14). It is an astonishing reality, fully grasped in the light of faith, yet historically attested to by those who were privileged to see the Risen Lord. It is a wondrous event which is not only absolutely unique in human history, but which lies *at the very heart of the mystery of time*. In fact, "all time belongs to [Christ] and all the ages," as the evocative liturgy of the Easter Vigil recalls in preparing the Paschal Candle. Therefore, in commemorating the day of Christ's Resurrection not just once a year but every Sunday, the Church seeks to indicate to every generation the true fulcrum of history, to which the mystery of the world's origin and its final destiny leads. It is right, therefore, to claim, in the words of a fourth century homily, that "the Lord's Day" is "the lord of days." Those who have received the grace of faith in the Risen Lord cannot fail to grasp the significance of this day of the week with the same deep emotion which led St. Jerome to say: "Sunday is the day of the Resurrection, it is the day of Christians, it is our day." For Christians, Sunday is "the fundamental feastday," established not only to mark the succession of time but to reveal time's deeper meaning.

— *Dies Domini*, Apostolic Letter, May 31, 1998

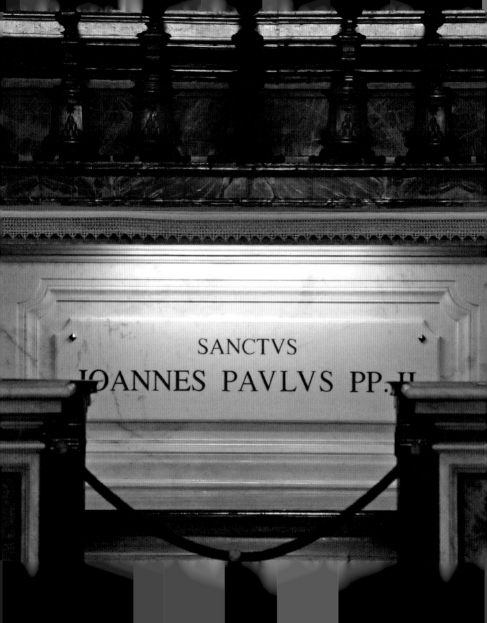

SECOND GLORIOUS MYSTERY

The Ascension of the Lord

*"As they were looking on, he was lifted up, and
a cloud took him from their sight."*

— Acts 1:9

Spiritual Fruit: For a firm hope and a great longing for heaven

Throughout his life, St. John Paul II had a deep love of and reverence for the Eucharist. "Every time we celebrate the Eucharist, we participate in the Lord's supper which gives us a foretaste of the heavenly glory," he said during a November 2004 Mass at St. Peter's Basilica, celebrated for the repose of the souls of cardinals and bishops who had died that year. John Paul knew that in the Eucharist earth unites with heaven, where Christ is seated at the Father's right hand. His life exhibited that faith, especially when, even in his advanced illness and infirmity, he insisted on celebrating the Mass publicly as a witness to all.

READ: ACTS 1:6–12
REFLECT WITH ST. JOHN PAUL II

In the providence of God — in the eternal design of the Father — the hour had come for Christ to go away. He would leave his Apostles behind, with his Mother Mary, but only after he had given them his instructions. The Apostles now had a mission to perform according to the instructions that Jesus left, and these instructions were in turn the faithful expression of the Father's will. The instructions indicated, above all, that the Apostles were to wait for the Holy Spirit, who was the gift of the Father. From the beginning, it had to be crystal-clear that the source of the Apostles' strength is the Holy Spirit. It is the Holy Spirit who guides the Church in the way of truth; the Gospel is to spread through the power of God, and not by means of human wisdom or strength. The Apostles, moreover, were instructed to teach — to proclaim the Good News to the whole world. And they were to baptize in the name of the Father, and of the Son, and of the Holy Spirit. Like Jesus, they were to speak explicitly about the Kingdom of God and about salvation. The Apostles were to give witness to Christ to the ends of the earth. The early Church clearly understood these instructions and the missionary era began. And everybody knew that this missionary era could never end until the same Jesus, who went up to heaven, would come back again.

— Homily, Solemnity of the Ascension, May 24, 1979

THIRD GLORIOUS MYSTERY

The Descent of the Holy Spirit
upon the Apostles and Mary

"And they were all filled with the holy Spirit and began to speak in different tongues, as the Spirit enabled them to proclaim."

— Acts 2:4

Spiritual Fruit: For holy wisdom that
we may know, taste, practice, and share

St. John Paul II was a prolific author, and throughout his life
he shared his wisdom with the world through written word.
These included numerous books, plays, and poems, as well as
fourteen papal encyclicals, fifteen apostolic exhortations, and doz-
ens of other documents. He knew the truth and yearned to share
it with the world. His bibliography is a treasure trove of truth for
the Church, part of the incredible legacy of this remarkable saint.

READ: ACTS 2:1–41
REFLECT WITH ST. JOHN PAUL II:

Veni, Sancte Spiritus! Thus beginning her invocation to the Holy
Spirit, the Church makes her own the substance of the Apostles'
prayer as they gathered with Mary in the Upper Room; indeed,
she extends it in history and makes it ever timely. *Veni, Sancte Spiritus!* Thus she says over and over in every corner of the earth, her
fervor unchanged, firmly aware that she must remain in the Upper Room, always awaiting the Spirit. At the same time, she knows

that she must leave the Upper Room and travel the world's roads, with the ever new task of bearing witness to the mystery of the Spirit. *Veni, Sancte Spiritus!* So we pray with Mary, sanctuary of the Holy Spirit, a most precious dwelling-place of Christ among us, so that she may help us to be living temples of the Spirit and tireless witnesses of the Gospel. *Veni, Sancte Spiritus! Veni, Sancte Spiritus! Veni, Sancte Spiritus! Amen!*

— Homily, Solemnity of Pentecost, May 31, 1998

FOURTH GLORIOUS MYSTERY

The Assumption of the Blessed Virgin Mary

"For he has looked upon his handmaid's lowliness; behold,
from now on will all ages call me blessed. ...
He has thrown down the rulers from their
thrones but lifted up the lowly."

— Luke 1:48–52

Spiritual Fruit: For the gift of true devotion to Mary, in order to live a good life and have a happy death

St. John Paul II had a lifelong devotion to the Blessed Mother, which became even stronger after the assassination attempt on his life on May 13, 1981. He credited Our Lady of Fatima, whose feast is observed on that date, with saving his life. "It was a mother's hand that guided the bullet's path," he would say later, after the two bullets that entered his abdomen struck no major organs. John Paul made three pilgrimages to Fatima over the course of his papacy, leaving in Mary's crown one of the bullets that struck him.

READ: 1 COR 15:20–27
REFLECT WITH ST. JOHN PAUL II

The first among those redeemed by Christ's paschal sacrifice, Mary shines forth today as Queen of us all, pilgrims on our way to immortal life. In her, assumed into heaven, we are shown the eternal destiny that awaits us beyond the mystery of death: a destiny of total happiness in divine glory. This supernatural vision sustains our daily pilgrimage. Mary teaches about life. By looking at her, we understand better the relative value of earthly greatness and the full sense of our Christian vocation. From her birth to her glorious Assumption, her life unfolded on a journey of faith, hope and charity. These virtues, which blossomed in a humble heart abandoned to God's will, are those adorning her precious, incorruptible crown as Queen. These are virtues which the Lord asks of all believers, if they are to share in his Mother's glory. ... Mary shines on earth "until the day of the Lord shall come, a sign of certain hope and comfort to the pilgrim People of God" (*Lumen Gentium*, No. 68). A caring mother to everyone, she supports the efforts of believers and encourages them to persevere in their commitment. ... Mary, Woman clothed with the sun, help us to fix our gaze on Christ amid the inevitable sufferings and problems of everyday life. Help us not to be afraid of following him to the very end, even when the cross seems unbearably heavy. Make us understand that this alone is the way which leads to the heights of eternal salvation. And from heaven, where you shine forth as Queen and Mother of mercy, watch over each one of your children. Guide them to love, adore and serve Jesus, the blessed fruit of your womb, O clement, O loving, O sweet Virgin Mary!

— Homily, Feast of the Assumption, August 15, 1997

FIFTH GLORIOUS MYSTERY

The Crowning of Mary
as Queen of Heaven and Earth

"A great sign appeared in the sky, a woman clothed with the sun, with the moon under her feet, and on her head a crown of twelve stars."

— Revelation 12:1

Spiritual Fruit: For perseverance and an increase in virtue up to the moment of our death and thereafter the eternal crown that is prepared for us

At Pope John Paul II's funeral in 2005, a crowd of mourners shouted "*santo subito*" — meaning "sainthood now!" Fewer than ten years later, on April 27, 2014, John Paul was canonized by Pope Francis in St. Peter's Square. Pope Francis said his saintly predecessor lived through the events of the twentieth century but was "not overwhelmed by them" — for "God was more powerful."

READ: REVELATION 12
REFLECT WITH ST. JOHN PAUL II

The Mother of Christ is glorified as "Queen of the Universe." She who at the Annunciation called herself the "handmaid of the Lord" remained throughout her earthly life faithful to what this name expresses. In this she confirmed that she was a true "disciple" of Christ, who strongly emphasized that his mission was one of service: "the Son of Man came not to be served but to serve, and to give his life as a ransom for many" (Mt 20:28). In this way Mary became the first of those who, "serving Christ also in others, with humility and patience lead their brothers and sisters to that King whom to serve is to reign," and she fully obtained that "state of royal freedom" proper to Christ's disciples: to serve means to reign!"

— *Redemptoris Mater*, No. 41, Encyclical, March 25, 1987

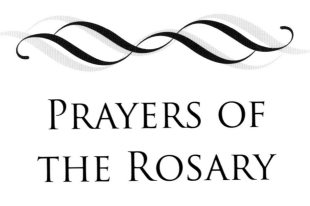

PRAYERS OF
THE ROSARY

Sign of the Cross

In the name of the Father, and of the Son, and of the Holy Spirit. Amen.

Apostles' Creed

I believe in God, the Father almighty, creator of heaven and earth; and in Jesus Christ, his only Son, our Lord; who was conceived by the Holy Spirit, born of the Virgin Mary, suffered under Pontius Pilate, was crucified, died, and was buried. He descended into hell; on the third day he rose again from the dead. He ascended into heaven and is seated at the right hand of God, the Father almighty; from thence he shall come to judge the living and the dead. I believe in the Holy Spirit, the holy catholic Church, the communion of saints, the forgiveness of sins, the resurrection of the body, and life everlasting. Amen.

Our Father

Our Father, who art in heaven, hallowed be thy name. Thy kingdom come. Thy will be done on earth, as it is in heaven. Give us this day our daily bread, and forgive us our trespasses, as we forgive those who trespass against us, and lead us not into temptation, but deliver us from evil. Amen.

Hail Mary

Hail Mary, full of grace. The Lord is with thee. Blessed art thou among women, and blessed is the fruit of thy womb, Jesus. Holy Mary, Mother of God, pray for us sinners, now and at the hour of our death. Amen.

Glory Be

Glory be to the Father, and to the Son, and to the Holy Spirit. As it was in the beginning, is now, and ever shall be, world without end. Amen.

Fátima Prayer

O my Jesus, forgive us our sins, save us from the fires of hell, lead all souls to heaven, especially those in most need of thy mercy. Amen.

Hail, Holy Queen

Hail, holy Queen, Mother of Mercy, our life, our sweetness, and our hope. To thee do we cry, poor banished children of Eve; to thee do we send up our sighs, mourning, and weeping in this valley of tears. Turn then, O most gracious advocate, thine eyes of mercy toward us, and after this, our exile, show unto us the blessed fruit of thy womb, Jesus. O clement, O loving, O sweet Virgin Mary.

V. Pray for us, O Holy Mother of God.

R. That we may be made worthy of the promises of Christ.

Concluding Rosary Prayer

Let us pray: O God, whose only begotten Son, by his life, death, and resurrection, has purchased for us the rewards of eternal life, grant, we beseech thee, that meditating upon these mysteries of the Most Holy Rosary of the Blessed Virgin Mary, we may imitate what they contain and obtain what they promise, through the same Christ our Lord. Amen.

PHOTO CAPTIONS

Page 18. Pope John Paul II greets the faithful at Zwyciestwa (Victory) Square, Warsaw, Poland, during his first pilgrimage to his homeland as pope on June 2, 1979. TEODOR WAL-CZAK/PICTURE-ALLIANCE /PAP/Newscom

Page 28. Pope John Paul II kisses the ground of his homeland on his arrival at the airport on June 2, 1979. PIPER/MIRRORPIX/Newscom

Page 32. Pope John Paul meets with his would-be assassin, Turkish gunman Mehmet Ali Ağca, in a cell of Rome's Rebibbia prison on December 27, 1983. Ağca, the man who shot the pope in 1981, was released from a Turkish jail in 2010. Ağca spent nineteen years in an Italian prison for the assassination attempt, but was freed in 2000 after a pardon at the pope's behest. He was then extradited to Turkey to serve a separate sentence in an Istanbul jail for robbery and murder. VATICAN/REUTERS/Newscom

Page 36. Pope John Paul II kisses a baby during the celebration of Corpus Domini (Body of the Lord) day in Rome on June 14, 2001. ALESSIA PIERDOMENICO/REUTERS/Newscom

Page 39. Pope John Paul II kisses a baby prior to his weekly general audience at the Vatican on November 28, 2001. PAOLO COCCO/REUTERS/Newscom

Page 40. File photo. OSV

Page 43. Pope John Paul II holds up a Rosary as he passes pilgrims in his Popemobile during a procession with five different stages corresponding to the five Mysteries of Light in Lourdes, France on August 14, 2004. The pope, calling himself a sick man among the sick, arrived at the world's premier Catholic miracle shrine and urged society not to cast aside the old and the suffering. REGIS DUVIGNAU/REUTERS/Newscom

Page 44. On the last day of his historic weeklong pilgrimage to the Holy Land, Pope John Paul II slips a prayer/message between two stones at the Western Wall also known as the Wailing Wall and begs God's forgiveness for the suffering of Jews throughout the world. GALAZKA/SIPA/Newscom

Page 50. Pope John Paul II looks over the Jordan River at one of the sites considered to be the place of Jesus' baptism. During his historic six-day visit, the pope advocated for peace and reconciliation among Jews, Christians, and Muslims. STR/REUTERS/Newscom

Page 54. Pope John Paul II blesses newlyweds on December 22, 1999, at the Vatican. Addressing magistrates, the Pope urged lawyers in Italy to shun divorce cases because marriage should be indissoluble and divine law supersedes human law. PAOLO COCCO/REUTERS/Newscom

Page 58. Pope John Paul II waves to the crowd from the Popemobile during his visit to Ireland in October 1979. STAFF/MIRRORPIX/Newscom

Page 62. File photo. OSV

Page 66. Pope John Paul II holds up the Host during a ceremony in St. Peter's Square marking the start of the 47th International Eucharistic Congress, one of the highlights of the Jubilee Year of 2000. The ceremony was attended by hundreds of religious brotherhoods representing their countries with typical processions and the carrying of crucifixes and statues of the Virgin. VINCENZO PINTO/REUTERS/Newscom

Page 72. Pope John Paul II prays in St. Peter's Basilica during a ceremony on April 21, 2002. PAOLO COCCO/REUTERS/Newscom

Page 76. Pope John Paul II after being shot by an assassin in St. Peter's Square on May 13, 1981. The pope was hit by two bullets fired by Mehmet Ali Ağca, a Turkish terrorist. KEYSTONE PICTURES USA/ZUMAPRESS/Newscom

Page 79. File photo. OSV

Page 80. Pope John Paul II in silent prayer on May 2, 1987, in the Basilica of the Kevelaer Shrine near the German-Netherlands border. WILHLEM LEUSCHNER/PICTURE-ALLIANCE / DPA/Newscom

Page 84. File photo. OSV

Page 88. Pope John Paul II prays inside the Church of the Holy Sepulchre, the site of Jesus' crucifixion, burial, and resurrection, during a visit to the Holy Land in March 2000. The stone is where Christ was laid to rest. VATICAN/REUTERS/Newscom

Page 94. Pope John Paul II holds a candle during the procession of the Easter Vigil celebrations in St. Peter's Square. VINCENZO PINTO/REUTERS/Newscom

Page 97. Pope John Paul II kisses the stone inside the Tomb of Jesus in the Church of the Holy Sepulchre during his visit to the Holy Land in March 2000. POOL/REUTERS/Newscom

Page 98. St. Peter's Basilica, tomb of St. John Paul II, Vatican City. MARIA LAURA ANTONELLI/SIPA/Newscom

Page 102. St. Peter's Basilica, Gian Lorenzo Bernini's Gloria above the Chair of St. Peter, Vatican City. RAIMUND KUTTER/BROKER/Newscom

Page 105. File photo. OSV

Page 106. File photo. OSV

Page 110. The crown of the Holy Mary of Fatima, containing a bullet that was aimed at Pope John Paul II in 1981, is displayed at the end of a procession in central Portugal on May 13, 2005. Fatima's pilgrimage season kicked off with a celebration that culminated exactly eighty-eight years after the Virgin Mary first appeared to three shepherd children there. JOSE MANUEL RIBEIRO/REUTERS/Newscom

Page 113. Pope John Paul II waves incense at the statue of the Madonna of Fatima, who he believes saved his life after a 1981 assassination attempt, during a celebration in St. Peter's Square on October 7, 2000. The pope had the statue brought to Rome from Fatima, Portugal, for a holy year celebration. The statue is a representation of the Madonna who appeared to three Portuguese shepherd children at Fatima in 1917. PAUL HANNA/REUTERS/ Newscom

Page 119. Pope John Paul II at a general audience in St. Peter's Square, June 1998. MONICA RICHERT HAMELL

ABOUT THE AUTHOR

Gretchen R. Crowe is editorial director for periodicals for Our Sunday Visitor, where she oversees the digital and print publication of *OSV Newsweekly*, *The Priest*, *Deacon Digest*, and *Simply Catholic*. An award-winning writer and photographer, Crowe has been a member of the Catholic Press Association since 2005. Crowe joined Our Sunday Visitor in March 2013 as *OSV Newsweekly* editor. She is also the author of *Why the Rosary, Why Now?* (OSV, 2017). Crowe lives in Indiana with her husband and two children.